the portable
She Calls Me Daddy

by
Robert Wolgemuth

Honor Books
Tulsa, Oklahoma

the portable She Calls Me Daddy
ISBN 1-56292-493-1
Copyright © 1998 by Robert Wolgemuth
330 Franklin Road
Suite 135-G
Brentwood, Tennessee 37027

Published by Honor Books
P.O. Box 55388
Tulsa, Oklahoma 74155

Introduction

Babies come in two kinds, boys and . . . girls. And when it's a girl, every dad in the world knows two things for sure: 1) She is going to be counting on him to be her daddy and 2) He has no idea what it's like to be a little girl! Most daddies need help . . . and they know it.

Well, put your anxieties to rest. I'm the daddy of two grown girls, and I'm so happy to be here to help you through this adventure. There are wonderful times to be had with a special little lady—your daughter. I guarantee that.

This portable edition is a condensation, based on my book, *She Calls Me Daddy*. If you want more insights on being your daughter's daddy, pick up the "unabridged" version at your favorite bookstore.

Contents

*The father of the [uncompromisingly] righteous
(the upright, in right standing with God)
shall greatly rejoice, and he who becomes
the father of a wise child shall have joy.*

PROVERBS 23:24 AMP

PROTECTION

Able to leap tall buildings

in a single bound!

Many *a father wishes he were*
strong enough to tear a telephone book in two —
especially if he has a teenage daughter.

— GUY LOMBARDO

Protection means to shield from
injury, harm, or danger.

It is difficult to give children a sense of security unless you have it yourself. If you have it, they catch it from you.

— DR. WILLIAM C. MENNINGER

I *owe almost everything to my father.*

— **MARGARET THATCHER**

The nature of your protection changes as your daughter grows.

Your job as a dad is to protect your daughter. When she's crawling toward a roaring fireplace, you yank her back. When her tricycle is heading for the street, you sprint down the driveway to stop it. And when you launch her into the hostile environment of growing up, you stand guard. Why? Because she needs it — and she wants it.

A *baby is God's opinion that the world should go on.*

— **C A R L S A N D B U R G**

Be attentive to the protection seesaw.

As she grows, her need for protection from physical dangers will diminish,
but her need for protection from emotional danger will increase.
When you're turning her away from the "sharp objects" and
"breakable figurines" of life, turn her attention to something else.
Saying, "Let's play a game!" or "How about a ride in Daddy's car?"
is a lot more effective than a constant "No-no-no."

It is a wise father that knows his own child.

— WILLIAM SHAKESPEARE

Turn loose on time. Learn to "let go" at the right pace.

If you overprotect, your daughter will develop an unhealthy, long-term
dependence on you. Then she won't learn to make her own good
decisions. She can't renew a driver's license or fill out an insurance form.
She won't drive a two-hour trip on her own. Don't let this happen.
Give your daughter a taste of independence when she's small.

Boundaries *protect and instruct.*

A child feels most secure when boundaries are given.

Heeding boundaries is important in your daughter's life.
Boundaries and restrictions do not disrupt life; they protect it.
Much like traffic signals, boundaries keep us from harm.

A *hug is a roundabout way of expressing emotion.*

— GIDEON WURDZ

She needs your emotional protection.

Emotional protection is far less visible or predictable than physical protection. It may change in form as the years go by, but it's just as important as physical protection. Be as available as you can. Always let your daughter's call through. Wear a pager or carry a cellular phone. If you're not there the moment she needs you, she'll find someone else — possibly someone whose wisdom is inferior to yours.

Time *as he grows old teaches many lessons.*

— **AESCHYLUS**

Don't delegate your role.

As a father, your role as the guiding and protecting point person in your daughter's life is a given. You can't delegate it to anyone else.
Your job as the protecting dad is irreplaceable.
You must know when to parent and protect and
when to step back and let your daughter learn a lesson.

Fathers give daughters away to other men
who aren't nearly good enough . . . so they can have
grandchildren that are smarter than anybody's.

— PAUL HARVEY

The big risk.

Fathering your daughter is a gamble.
It's about long shots and holding your breath.
About doing your best, then hoping, believing, and praying —
especially praying.

CONVERSATION

Just keep talking!

To talk to a child, to fascinate her, is much
more difficult than to win an electoral victory.
But it is also more rewarding.

— COLETTE

*Conversation means building bridges
of communication for a lifetime.*

B*lessed indeed is the man who hears*
many gentle voices call him father!

— LYDIA M. CHILD

The first duty of love is to listen.

— PAUL TILLICH

In order to converse, one must also listen.

Give your girl the gift of conversational skills. No interrupting.
Just listen with focus and make eye contact. Try to see a situation
from your child's point of view. When your daughter is young,
her perspective will be undeveloped. She won't know as much as
you know. Don't assume she's more sophisticated in her reasoning or
thought process even though she may stand as tall as you. If she tells
you something that doesn't make sense to you, ask for clarification.

Every speaker has a mouth;
An arrangement rather neat.
Sometimes it's filled with wisdom.
Sometimes it's filled with feet.

— ROBERT ORBEN

Talk about feelings.

As you learn to protect her delicate emotions, learn to ask about them.
"How did that make you feel?" is a magic question. Always support
her answer, too, whether she feels angry or hurt. Tell her, "If that
had happened to me, I would probably be angry (or hurt), too."
Never argue with her feelings. You'll shut her down,
and she'll stop talking to you.

W*hen communication stops, abnormality sets in.*

— E D W I N   L O U I S   C O L E

Young lovebirds usually choose between conversation and the backseat.

As she begins to discover the world of other men besides you, she'll be able to make better judgments about who's compatible as a potential friend and who's not. Because she has learned the art of good conversation, your daughter will also be less likely to get caught in compromising physical situations.

A torn jacket is soon mended;
but hard words bruise the heart of a child.

— HENRY WADSWORTH LONGFELLOW

Apologize for words poorly spoken.

Because you're normal, you're going to say the wrong thing at the wrong
time. You're going to hurt people's feelings, including your daughter's.
Show her what it sounds like to hear her dad correct his words,
and if necessary, ask her forgiveness for the error.

Words have an awesome impact.
The impressions made by a father's voice
can set in motion an entire trend of life.

— GORDON MACDONALD

The father-daughter relationship lasts a lifetime.

The ability and desire of your daughter to talk with you about her life and feelings when she is grown begins in her childhood. Conversation forms the bond that will be the foundation of your friendship later in life.

But words are things, and a small drop of ink,
Falling like dew, upon a thought, produces
That which makes thousands, perhaps millions, think.

— LORD BYRON

The power of words.

Show your daughter that words are wonderful. Read to
your girl even before you think she can understand a thing.
It will create in her a love for words and an appreciation for
your bringing the world to her through books.

A *wise man's heart guides his mouth,*
and his lips promote instruction.

PROVERBS 16:23 NIV

Once spoken, words can never be unsaid.

Words have unbelievable power. Words restore and renew people.
They lift the heart and heal the spirit. They can build the character of
the speaker and the esteem of the recipient. Unfortunately, they can
also cause great pain. The tongue is like a rudder of a ship. With just
a little instrument, an entire life can be set on the right course
or perilously aimed at an iceberg.

Cold words freeze people, and hot words scorch them, and bitter words make them bitter, and wrathful words make them wrathful. Kind words also produce their own image on the soul, and a beautiful image it is. They soothe, and quiet, and comfort the hearer.

— BLAISE PASCAL

Conversation is magic.

Conversation used properly can release the pressure that builds in every
relationship. It is the magic device that gives people the opportunity to
talk about frustrations or fears without allowing pressure to
build, to explode, and to harm irreparably.

H*e that converses not, knows nothing.*

— **T H O M A S F U L L E R**

Talk openly.

In every situation you encounter with your daughter,
your ability to openly talk about it will be the greatest guiding device
you could employ. If your daughter feels free to talk to you about
what's really going on in her life, she'll stay out of
serious trouble most of the time.

AFFECTION

Daddy, hold me!

Praise is well, compliment is well, but affection —
that is the last and final and most precious reward
that any man can win.

— MARK TWAIN

Affection means responding with a hug
whenever she really needs it —
whether she actually asks for one or not.

I *am only one,*
But still I am one.
I cannot do everything.
But I can do something.
And because I cannot do everything
I will not refuse to do
The something that I can do.

— EDWARD E. HALE

Affection is responsible for nine-tenths of whatever solid and durable happiness there is in our lives.

— C . S . L E W I S

To your daughter, touching is the key to her heart.

Hold your daughter when she's a baby, and stroke her face
with your hand. Hold her hand when you walk with her.
Visit her room just before she goes to sleep, and kiss her good night.
Hug her with your whole arms — wrap her up like a blanket.
Let her heart know that she is absolutely secure in her daddy's arms.

Kind words can be short and easy to speak,
but their echoes are truly endless.

— MOTHER TERESA

Affirm the person, not the performance.

Pouring affection on your daughter will bring her and you
a great deal of joy and pave the way in building and shaping
her character. Later on, she'll give you permission to
be tough when her heart knows you've been tender.

Nothing has a better effect
upon children than praise.

— SIR PHILIP SIDNEY

Write and speak your "touching words."

Touching words are statements of affection, whether written or spoken.
Leave notes everywhere. Notes left on pillows and tucked into shoes
and suitcases are powerful word "touchings." Take time to speak your
verbal affections in a slowing-down moment. But do not exaggerate.
When you speak kind and affectionate words to your girl,
don't say things you both know are untrue. For the moment,
that might feel good, but in time she will realize it's not true.

Touching words only work if you have your daughter's
undivided attention and you carefully speak each word.

Be kind to thy father, for when thou wert young,
Who loved thee so fondly as he?
He caught the first accents that fell from thy tongue,
And joined in thy innocent glee.

— **M A R G A R E T   C O U R T N E Y**

Start a tradition.

Special occasions throughout the year offer many opportunities to begin.
On Father's Day write your daughter a letter telling her the joy *you*
feel being her dad. Remember your daughter on Valentine's Day,
and give her a special Christmas gift just from you each year.

Every word and deed of a parent is a fiber woven
into the character of a child that ultimately determines
how that child fits into the fabric of society.

— DAVID WILKERSON

Show your love.

Studies have proven that infants can die and children fail to thrive
when deprived from physical touch. Psychologists say everyone
needs at least four hugs a day. A gentle touch or hug may be
the only way to communicate at an awkward time
or painful moment when words escape you.

Security is stability within ourselves.

— **B E R N A R D   M .   B A R U C H**

The security of your arms.

Give your daughter the enveloping security of your physical and
emotional arms. She must know your tender touch and your affirming
words. These must come from you at times when there's
no direct connection between her conduct
and your loving support.

The greatest thing a father can do for his children is love their mother.

— **J O S H   M C D O W E L L**

Demonstrate affection to your wife in front of your daughter.

As you demonstrate love and affection to your daughter,
don't forget that loving her mother is even more important.
Your daughter will catch a firsthand glimpse of what it's like
to be in a loving relationship with a man.

The purest affection the heart can hold is
the honest love of a nine-year-old.

— HOLMAN DAY

She needs fewer things and more of you.

Recognize that doing generous things is good,
but it's not the same as genuine affection.

Some dads may be uncomfortable with conscientiously
showing affection on a daily basis. It's tempting and easier
to just be extra generous on birthdays and Christmas.
That's nice, but it's not going to get the job done.

DISCIPLINE

A sledgehammer,
a couple of crowbars,
and a level?

If all our wishes were gratified,
most of our pleasures would be destroyed.

— RICHARD WHATELY

D iscipline means to "build" a daughter
who is self-controlled and whose
interior structure is straight and true.

When I start a building project, I always take
a sledge hammer, a couple of crowbars, and a level.
These tools make a lot of noise and can be a pain to use,
but if you eventually want your wallpaper
to hang correctly, you need to be sure that
the insides of your walls are squared up.

Authority without wisdom is like a heavy ax
without an edge, fitter to bruise than polish.

— **ANNE BRADSTREET**

Be tough and tender.

Be the most affirming and tender dad you've ever heard of,
and be the most no-nonsense, strict father on the planet.

Define the rules and consistently enforce them. Discipline must be swift,
painful, and fair, but never rash or in a rage. Waiting too long between
the infraction and the penalty diminishes the impact of the punishment.
A consequence that isn't painful is not a consequence at all.
And when the sentence doesn't match the severity of the crime,
it will be seen as unfair and will lose its impact.

Discipline is its own reward.

Balance the positive with the negative.

Life must include the positive and the negative to be in balance.
We tend to believe that positive is always good and negative is always bad.
Anything truly worthwhile contains both — including life.

Discipline puts back in its place
that something in us which should
serve but wants to rule.

— A CARTHUSIAN

Discipline includes both pain and joy.

The achievement of personal discipline can be a great thrill all by itself.
It doesn't even have to accomplish anything useful
to have significant value.

Praise publicly, punish privately.

If you embarrass your daughter, shame on you.

Like yelling, creating embarrassment focuses pain on the wrong thing.
Disciplining your daughter is an intimate and secret thing.
Don't do it in public. If you embarrass your daughter,
you *must* apologize to her, which doesn't do much
for the lesson she's suppose to be learning.

The way I see it,
if you want the rainbow,
you gotta put up with the rain.

— DOLLY PARTON

Set the guidelines.

Talk about the guidelines, then hold your breath and hope for the best.
Your ability to talk through issues, explaining why you've decided to set
certain guidelines, will help to keep your home free from outbreaks of
hostility. And if you decide to hold the line on certain things,
don't expect your daughter to applaud your every decision.

Let the punishment match the offense.

— CICERO

Discipline must be fair.

Fairness in disciplining means that the punishment should match the crime. Give her a dose of real life consequences. For example, if your daughter leaves a mess, make her clean it up. If she hurts her friend, make her apologize. Fair punishment is one of the most important "gifts" you'll ever give your daughter.

A *man must be big enough to admit his mistakes,*
smart enough to profit from them,
and strong enough to correct them.

— JOHN MAXWELL

Take time out for some perspective.

Don't haul off and blast your daughter the moment she steps out of line.
Take a deep breath to calm down. You're trying to teach her something,
not taking an opportunity to blow off steam or get even.

LAUGHTER

Did you hear the

one about . . . ?

L*aughter is the shortest distance*
between two people.

— **VICTOR BORGE**

Laughter means taking time to
see the humor in life and being willing to
poke a little fun at yourself.

L*aughter is a smile that burst.*

— **PATRICIA NELSON**

Nothing I've ever done has given me more
joys and rewards than being
a father to my children.

— BILL COSBY

Be fun to live with.

Life is sometimes too serious. Tell your daughter stories
about your childhood, even your worst foibles. Don't be afraid to
laugh at yourself. Cartoonists and humorists are always poking fun
at themselves and at life. Your life is full of the same kinds of experiences.
Laugh at yourself and laugh at your circumstances.

Happiness is inward, and not outward; and so,
it does not depend on what we have,
but on what we are.

— HENRY VAN DYKE

Spend quality time together.

Avoid the temptation to always watch television together.
That does little to enhance your ability to interact. Play games —
everything from store-bought board games and puzzles
to imaginative games on a road trip.

Far too many adults I know are serious as a heart attack. They live with their fists tightened, and they die with deep frowns. They cannot remember when they last took a chance or risked trying something new. The last time they tried something really wild, they were nine years old. I ask you, where's the fun?

— CHARLES SWINDOLL

Chill.

Ask yourself every once in a while,
"Am I fun to live with?"
What a good thing to do!

History *is the study of other people's mistakes.*

— **PHILIP GUEDALLA**

Retell the stories that last a lifetime.

Remember the situations you got yourself into when you were young.
They make great material for passing on life's lessons.
Reminisce with your daughter about those fateful experiences.
She'll see that even the most difficult times will pass. It's great fun, too.

Laughter is sunshine in a house.

— WILLIAM M. THACKERY

Remember the three rules for laughter:

1. Laugh *with* your girl, never *at* her.
2. Laugh at your own past experiences or circumstances.
3. Laugh at yourself. You'll survive!

The thing to remember about fathers is, they're men.
A girl has to keep it in mind:
They are dragon-seekers, bent on improbable rescues.
Scratch any father, you find

Someone chock-full of qualms and romantic terrors,
Believing change is a threat —
Like your first shoes with heels on, like your first bicycle
It took such months to get.

— **PHYLLIS MCGINLEY**

The best and most beautiful things in
the world cannot be seen or even touched.
They must be felt with the heart.

— HELEN KELLER

Laugh!

Laugh with your girl. Be silly.
Fill your home with joy.

FAITH

Jesus loves me,
this I know . . .

The great door sighs, then opens, and a child
enters the church and kneels at the front pew.
The Maker of the Universe has smiled.
He made the church for this one interview.

— DANIEL SARGENT

Faith means knowing in your heart
that Jesus loves you.

I_f a child lives with security,
she learns faith.

— **DOROTHY LAW NOLTE**

*C*hildren are likely to live up to
what you believe of them.

— LADY BIRD JOHNSON

Make your faith normal.

Your task is to help your little girl grow into
a well-balanced woman who loves God.

One of the most important things you can do is to make your faith
normal. Talk about God as though knowing Him is a simple fact, not
something mysterious or puzzling. Make it part of the daily routine.
Let your daughter see you treat your love for God as part of your
normal activity — not some clumsy diversion from real life.

The way you honor the God who has authority over
you will give your daughter a pattern to follow
when it comes to her respect for the daddy
who has authority over her.

Celebrate your faith.

Teach your daughter to pray. Teach your daughter to praise.
Teach your daughter to sing.

When you and your daughter are talking to or about God,
you are literally referring to the eternal Creator of the universe.
Remind her of God's majesty by an occasional mention of
His creative genius. Give your daughter an awe for God.

W_e should seize every opportunity to give
encouragement. Encouragement is oxygen to the soul.

— GEORGE M. ADAMS

Build godly character in your daughter.

Thank God for the miracle of your daughter's birth, and
publicly promise to nurture her. Verbally bless her.
Teach her to give. Read the Bible together.
Give your daughter an extended Christian family.

If you have no prayer life yourself,
it is rather a useless gesture to make
your child say prayers every night.

— **PETER MARSHALL**

Let her teach you about faith.

Helping to build a solid faith in your daughter will have
a profound influence on your own faith. As she gets older,
you'll discover why Jesus commended the little children for
the depth of their faith, because she will teach you!

Go to a bookstore and buy a child's Bible for
your daughter — even if she's too young to read.
Tell her that this book is all hers. Have her name
stamped on the cover if you can. Plant the truth of
God's word deep in her soul when she's a tiny girl.

Sometimes less is more.

When you're driving along with your daughter on one of your weekend errands, say something like, "Oh honey, look at that beautiful tree. Isn't God wonderful?" No references to your minister's sermon on Sunday will be necessary. This is enough.

The best teacher of children . . . is one
who is essentially childlike.

— HENRY LOUIS MENCKEN

Give your daughter an opportunity to teach.

Encourage your daughter, as soon as she's old enough, to volunteer
to help in a nursery or Sunday school class. She'll find herself on
the receiving end of honest inquiries about life. And relationships.
And God. As she answers those inquisitive little minds,
she will be sealing her own ideas about such things.

A *family that prays together stays together.*

— **KATHRYN SPINK**

Teach your daughter to pray.

Teaching your daughter to talk to God is critical to her building
a meaningful relationship with Him. One of the best times to
help your child pray is at bedtime. Make it a nightly ritual.
How touching to hear your child bring her most
important concerns boldly to God's attention!

CONDUCT

You be the judge.

When you go out into the world,
watch out for traffic, hold hands,
and stick together.

— ROBERT FULGHUM

Conduct means deciding what is appropriate behavior,
setting guidelines, and communicating
with your daughter before, during,
and after certain situations arise.

*The child that never learns to obey
her parents in the home will not obey
God or man out of the home.*

— SUSANNE WESLEY

A word is dead
When it is said,
Some say.

I say it just
Begins to live
That day.

— **EMILY DICKINSON**

Correct conduct is a by-product.

Protection, conversation, affection, correction, laughter,
and faith should precede an emphasis on conduct.
Even if you have a high-spirited strong-willed girl,
setting rules for conduct should be your *last* concern —
after you've laid the appropriate groundwork.

To be an effective parent, you must let your children
know what you expect from them, and
then you must be close enough to the action
to be able to regularly inspect their work.

— ZIG ZIGLAR

No Surprises!

Whatever they are, make sure your daughter understands the rules.
No surprises or changes in mid-course. Your success as a father will
depend on your ability to communicate clearly what is right and
your diligence in making sure your daughter is following up.
Make sure your guidelines are clearly defined.

If you tell the truth,
you don't have to remember anything.

— **MARK TWAIN**

Living with truth.

Let your daughter know that dishonesty is absolutely unacceptable.
A person who grows up not fully appreciating the importance of
truth-telling is a person bound to live a painful life. A father must
teach his daughter honesty and practice it himself.
Suppose a father respectfully tells his daughter
to be truthful, but when the phone rings, he calls out to her,
"Tell them I'm not home." The message is clear.
If your girl is taught to lie for you, she will lie to you.

You have the right — even an obligation —
to tell your daughter that something she's wearing could
"communicate" the wrong thing to a boy.

Avoid extremes.

You don't want your daughter to get her identity from what she wears.
Ultimately, you want her to be known by her character.
Although it's easy to notice only when your daughter is
wearing something "questionable," be quick to tell her
how wonderful she looks when she's wearing something conservative.
An honest compliment from a boy (you) will be highly motivating to her.

Honor *is purchased by the deeds we do.*

— CHRISTOPHER MARLOWE

Teach your daughter about money and its value when she's young.

There are only three uses for money:

1. *Spending* is for living today.
2. *Saving* is for living tomorrow.
3. *Giving* makes everyone happy.

M usic is the universal language of mankind.

— HENRY WADSWORTH LONGFELLOW

Teach your daughter to sing and enjoy music.

Start with simple songs when she's young. Music is going to be an important part of your daughter's life. It's the language of her generation, symbolizing the thinking of a culture. So when she's young, give her some of the really good stuff. It will help her as she makes musical judgments later.

Encourage a balance of musical styles. Play a variety of music in your home. Take her to the symphony or opera. Let her hear the type of music you grew up listening to. And respect her taste in music as well. When you're in the car together, let her choose the radio station once in a while.

Experience is a good school,
but the fees are high.

— HEINRICH HEINE

Talk openly about the unhappy results of past foolishness.

Your experiences provide a helpful backdrop for insisting on good
conduct. To illustrate the inescapable truths of cause and effect,
draw on your own experiences. There's no need to go into
the sordid details, however. Let her draw her own conclusions.
It makes a stronger impact if she has to think about it herself.

A *place for everything and . . .*
everything in its place.

— HENRY G. BOHN

Remove the evidence.

Although it's true no one ever died of a messy room,
the thing about living in a family is that one person's thoughtfulness
will often affect someone else. If someone walks into a room
and can tell your child has been in there, ask your child
to go back and remove the evidence.

A *father's words are like a thermostat that sets the temperature in the house.*

— PAUL LEWIS

Curfew time should not be a hard-and-fast rule.

Every situation creates its own be-home-by time.
Just be sure you've established that time in advance.
And set this guideline: she *always* calls if she
can't make it by the curfew. Be consistent.

THE INVESTMENT OF A LIFETIME

It begins with the first tender,

loving gaze into your

daughter's eyes.

That which we persist in doing becomes easier —
not that the nature of the task has changed,
but our ability to do has increased.

— RALPH WALDO EMERSON

Gentlemen, try not to become men of success.
Rather, become men of value.

— ALBERT EINSTEIN

Begin with the end in mind.

Being the father of a girl can be a journey into the great unknown.
The greatest challenge you'll face as the father of a daughter is to keep
from being distracted by the day-to-day stuff — the little duties
and challenges that can easily capture a dad's full-time attention.
Picture what it is you're "building" here: a healthy, poised,
confident, balanced, and happy woman — a complete daughter
who will someday be counted among your closest friends.

Failure is the opportunity to begin again,
more intelligently.

— HENRY FORD

Things usually take longer than we had planned.

Starting a project is easy, finishing it is another matter.
That takes perseverance. It can be difficult to see a project through
to completion. When being a father stops being fun, it's easy to
walk away or quit. But don't let go, you can't quit. Raising your girl
will take about 20 years to finish. It's going to take longer than
you think, and you've got to make it the whole way to the end.

If a father feels bewildered and even defeated,
let him take comfort from the fact that
whatever he does in any fathering has a
50 percent chance of being right.

— BILL COSBY

Your daughter is a free agent.

You're dealing with a person who has her own agenda, her own mind
and will. Nothing you can do will ever force her into a certain kind of
thinking or behavior. There are no guarantees, no risk-free formulas.
Ultimately, she'll think and do what she decides to think and do.
However, you can and should create an environment
that promotes her best shot at success.

You can either take action, or you can hang back
and hope for a miracle. Miracles are great,
but they are so unpredictable.

— PETER DRUCKER

Push ahead.

No one is perfect, not even a father. Resist the temptation to quit —
the payoff is well worth the sacrifice. When you blow it with your daughter
(and you will sometimes), be quick to apologize and ask for her forgiveness.
You may sometimes pray, "Lord give me patience, and give it to me right
now!" Sometimes you may feel like a failure and want to quit. But ask
the Lord to help you be a loving, gracious, enduring, and patient dad.

What lies behind us and what lies before us are tiny matters compared to what lies within us.

— OLIVER WENDELL HOLMES

Teach by your example.

Life goes beyond technique and style. Our true success
will only come from what's inside. Here's a sobering thought:
Your success as a dad has far more to do with who you are than with
how well you're able to do certain things with and for your daughter.
Ultimately, she'll learn more by watching you than by listening to you —
more from your example than from your teaching techniques.

Never underestimate the importance and impact of honor.
A dad taking time to honor his daughter with his love and his time,
teaches her to honor and respect him. He helps her understand
the importance of honoring God and others.

You *can never plan the future by the past.*

— EDMUND BURKE

Spend less time looking back and more time looking ahead.

It's never too late. Someone has described the past as hardened concrete and the future as wet cement. Rather than filling your mind with what you could have or should have done, focus on what you can do from this point on. Recommit yourself to being the best dad you can possibly be.

It matters not what you are thought to be,
but what you are.

— LATIN PROVERB

And finally . . .

Never stop working on yourself. If the truth be known, you and I are constantly doing battle with appropriate versus inappropriate behavior. As you work on improving yourself, be open to your daughter about the challenges you're facing. She may let you in on her own challenges.

Be quick to provide encouragement.

Life is not a destination; it's a journey.

About the Author

Writer, speaker, and publishing executive **Robert Wolgemuth** counts being the daddy of two now-grown daughters among his greatest accomplishments.

He has been in the publishing business for 20 years, including as a marketing executive in magazine and book publishing in Illinois, Texas, and Tennessee. In 1992, he co-founded a talent management agency, of which he currently serves as chairman. He formerly served as president of the Evangelical Christian Publishers' Association.

He and his wife, Bobbie, live in Brentwood, Tennessee, and his daughters, Julie and Missy, are in their 20s.

Additional copies of this book are available from your local bookstore.

Look for Robert Wolgemuth's upcoming portable
Pray with Me Daddy
coming soon to a bookstore near you.

Honor Books
Tulsa, Oklahoma